Superbloom

Requiem for My Sister

Superbloom

Requiem for My Sister

by

Joyce Schmid

Cover design by Shay Culligan
Cover image by Anastasia Iunosheva, licensed from iStock,
image number1294232837.jpg
Black and white flower image by Anh Lee on Unsplash
Author photo by Chris Conroy Photography,
Mountain View, California

ISBN: 979-8-90146-724-4
Library of Congress Control Number: 2026935539

Kelsay Books
502 South 1040 East, A-119
American Fork, Utah 84003
Kelsaybooks.com

Praise for *Superbloom*

Superbloom, an elegy for and love letter to a fragile, brilliant younger sister, tells a story that is at once heartbreaking and beautiful, universal and one of a kind. Weaving together lyric fragments, family memories, and flashes of astonishing clarity, these poems trace the evolution of a sisterly bond shaped by beauty, rivalry, mental illness and all that entails—the luminous moments from a shared childhood, the envy, fears, distances, and confusions, the slow erosion of memory, and finally, the love.

Finding grace in grief, Schmid brings tenderness, even wonder to these poems. Every page is a surprise and a revelation, moving seamlessly from the simple and the direct *(And now you're dying in your brain, / the place where you had always tried to live.)* to the mysterious and the metaphoric. *(You say, 'I love you, love you, love you' / and the squirrel's feet are seared to blisters),* while being always, always achingly, bracingly precise. She writes, *The air is colorless, / we barely notice it when it is clean— / we breathe unconsciously, ungratefully. / My sister was like air to me.*

What Schmid has accomplished here is remarkable. Interweaving lines from her sister's unpublished poems, she has created in *Superbloom* a final collaboration—an echo across time.

—Paula Stacey, editor, *Poetry International*

A gorgeous requiem for the poet's sister, Joyce Schmid's *Superbloom* brims with the abundance its title suggests. Resisting any too easy answer to suffering and loss, Schmid nevertheless employs her formidable lyric gifts to join grief with amazement, to make a lasting and vivid place for "the soul blown open."

—Peter Campion, author, *Radical as Reality: Form and Freedom in American Poetry* (University of Chicago Press)

Acknowledgments

Deepest thanks to the editors of the following journals where these poems first appeared, sometimes in earlier versions.

Chaffin Journal: "The Tracks"

Five Points: "Cremation"

Flying South: "Street Games," "Floodlit"

Hole in the Head Review: "Celebration of Life"

Lake Effect: "Poison" (as "Little Sister")

Newtown Literary: "Foreshadows" (as "Ash Trees")

Northwest Review: "Even the Air"

The Orchards Poetry Journal: "*Even myself reminds me of you*" (as "To My Sister")

Passager: "Superbloom," "*Into the raw mottled air of a dim bedroom,*" "Aran Sweater," "Things to Not Say," "Dialogue with My Sister's Poems on the First Anniversary of Her Death"

Watershed Review: "I Wouldn't Have Believed It Either"

Contents

Even the Air

. . . even the air is independable . . .
—HD

Lavender,
why are you straining toward me?
I am not the sun.
Day lily,
I have no reprieve.

And you, my little sister,
when you grasped at me that day
as to a tree-branch jutting from the shore,
I didn't know
the rapids overwhelming you

were real
and you were really
being swept away.

Street Games

Bellerose, N.Y.

Remember how we threw a pink Spaldeen
against the sidewalk, caught it, threw it down again,
while singing *A my name is Alice*
and my husband's name is Al?
We turned our right leg over every name.

Jumping rope, we chanted,
Wrap her up in tissue paper, send her down the elevator,
see how long the baby can sleep.
The words came spinning down to us in seed-pods
from the maple trees. We picked them up
and stuck the polynoses on our noses.

Now that we are old
and you are dying
I think about that elevator shaft,
that baby wrapped in tissue paper,
tossed away.

The Tracks

no playing on the tracks of course we did
in titillating terror
Raymond McEvoy and Michael Burns
and you and me back in the days

when Raymond had a cellarful of coal
and endless freight trains
with their smoke and whistles
tore out from one nowhere to another
because there wasn't anywhere but there

no freight trains any more in Bellerose
even the tracks themselves are gone
there's just a tiny rise with grass and silence
where the frightful freight trains roared

Poison

The '47 Blizzard drifted high and almost ate you whole,
until they found you, cold and even more ethereal, but safe.
This happened in a place where nothing grew but crabgrass,

and they poisoned it because it came up wild.
They beat the wildness out of children too,
but not you, little sister.

You were thin and couldn't eat.
They combed your pale hair tight,
as smooth as soap, so taut it must have hurt.

Your poems flew like luna moths
and burned up in the light,
they were so delicate and green.

Now, like Penelope, you tear your words apart each night,
waiting for your death to come and claim you,
bewildered, rising from your chair.

Sonnet in Green

Little sister—you were prettier than me,
you floated through the living room,
your feet not touching earth, your azure eyes
near-blind without the glasses you refused to wear—
I swear that we could see right through you
just as if you weren't there, but you were there all right,
your pale hair falling in your face, a paragon of grace.
I slunk around like Gollum, riddled through with jealousy:
the ones who brought me here
did not love me, they loved you—
almost non-existent thing, no barrier to light—
the one who sank to rest when not in use,
the one I hated most,
the one who loved me best.

Off to College Together

Steam huffed around the train,
and when it cleared,
the wheels were drumming paradiddles,

grass was rushing, trees were streaking,
and Long Island Sound was sprouting sails.
The train was our cocoon,

and by the time we reached South Station,
our metamorphosis complete,
we flew.

The Boston Kitchen Ladies

The Boston kitchen ladies
were a little sharp, a little cross,
and yet they brought a Mason jar for us
wrapped up in tissue and red string
the Christmas that we stayed at school—
a jar of applesauce, home-made,
a little tart, with chunks of apple in it.

Today in California,
it's a Boston-autumn day. No sun.
The stores are twinkly with early Christmas things.
I wish we could go back
and find those ladies with their clucking frowns,
and try to hug them as they back away,
and tell them it was warm beneath their wings.

Foreshadows

You visited to comfort me when my friend Evie died.
Her children lived without her in her house
where once her own old mother came to die
when we were young and had no time to cry.
The shadows of the leaves were omens over her.
That was when it used to rain,
when everything was green and wet
beneath a canopy of ash trees,
branches swaying, creaking, warning us,
before we ever thought a drought
could shrivel up the pines, could stop the waterfalls
and leave the granite cliffs dry-eyed,
before the forests up and down the golden state
were burning.

Into the raw mottled air of a dim bedroom

—Lucie Brock-Broido

Your love is focused in so tight
it's burning holes in the upholstery.
The smoke is everywhere, it smells like need.

You say, *I'm weary with my groaning; all the night*
make I my bed to swim; I'm watering my couch with tears.
All day you pace, no place to sit.

Your world has shrunk to just a body
no quetiapine, no Prozac, no alprazolam can fix.
Your Positron Emission scan is blue—

the color of your eyes, the color of despair.
Outside, a bird that loves you
perches, folds its wings, and sings,

I will not leave you comfortless, I'll come to you.

Mosquito Dream

You sip my blood,
antennae trembling,
your wings and body delicately drawn
in 9H pencil.

I could spare
the drop you drink
but my unthinking fingers
squash you.

As you fade, you say,

I'm not a mosquito,
I'm a concept in your mind—

you—my little sister—
three years old—
balanced tiptoe
on the footboard
of your bed
your right arm straining to the lamp
a bit too high—
but reaching it
and switching off
the light.

Across the Telephone Wire

Does the squirrel running on the phone line
feel the conversations underneath—
you telling me, "We used to live with students,"
meaning that your daughter and her family moved out,
informing me your husband is a different Bob
although he looks the same,
imploring as you pace from room to room,
"When can I go home?"

You say, "I love you, love you, love you"
and the squirrel's feet are seared to blisters
by your need; he runs into the walnut tree
and hides. The walnuts clatter
on the Santa Clara Valley clay
just as my pearls bounced on a hard
indifferent floor the night my necklace broke.
I didn't know their worth, that they were real,
gestated in a living flesh that died for me.

By My Eyes There Passes / the Gold Where the Dust of My Childhood Dances

—Rocío Ágreda Piérola (Tr. Jessica Sequeira)

I try to touch your blowing-flowing voile of veil
as you run lightly toward the asphodel,

not far away now—meadows of it
waiting for your feet.

So effortless, your dance—
like water falling back to ocean with no plan but rest.

However hard I sing, you will not stay.
All I can do is watch you dance away, away.

Long Distance

Pandemic, 2020–22

Often, you are mad at him
who cleans and shops

and chauffeurs you around
and cooks you two full meals a day.

Your daughter visits twice a week
and tries to wrest you from dementia's maw.

And I
who couldn't extricate our mother

from her life-long grief
can only phone you from another state,

trying not to lose
my tenderness.

Compassion Fatigue

Sister with your disappearing mind,
your pain is sculpting pathways in my brain,
and maybe the priest was right to say

the greatest enemy of love
is self-preservation.

Again I dreamed
there was a baby in the house.
Again I had no milk.

I'm sitting in an armchair,
staring at my screen. One touch,
and everything's for sale.

What product can I order to exfoliate
my heart?

Close of Day

A sunset falling onto sharpened peaks,
spring blossoms tearing from the trees,
but unlike them, you feel the pain.

Do not go gentle, sister.

How can such small bones
contain such fear?
Frozen at your door,

you clutch the lifeline of my hand,
too terrified to step into a world
that you no longer understand.

I want to give you courage to protest,
to scratch the sky with feral fingernails,
to snatch the flowers high

before they reach the ground,
but I retreat from your demands, your screams.
I can't unhear my own unwelcome prayer:

gentle, oh go gentle, sister.

Floodlit

As a girl, you made up plays,
yourself director, editor, and star,
princess of a cast of china statuettes.
Your inch-wide headboard was our stage.
We'd kneel with you behind your bed
and reach to slide the figures back and forth
across their narrow wooden world
for our imagined audience.
Summon the princess to my royal bed.
We'd speak your lines, but there were no asides.
Out of the game . . . we'd beg, and you,
in princess voice, would answer us: *What game?*

You were to write *I cringe to bare my being in a public place . . .*
I will] pretend I am alone . . . more private
in imagined privacy. For you, it was a choice
to live or not live in reality.

You married your first husband young,
beside him when he got his PhD at twenty-three in Math.
You wrote to him, *You've made your life and mine so real to me,*
That I'm made subject to reality,
but then took off your glasses, left him,
and went off to Hollywood.

You opted not to see. You just unveiled your eyes—
blue, beautiful, with flecks of gold.

And now you're dying in your brain,
the place where you had always tried to live.
You say "*They're feeding me unholy water.*"
You say "*Goodbye—I'm needed on the set.*"

Does Light Emerge from the Other Side of a Singularity, Creating New Worlds?

You phone in agony. You've known
for months the man who says
he is your husband is a multiplicity
of men named Bob, but now
your house is all in pieces too.
I tell you that the problem is your brain:
you need a rest, some dinner
and a bath. For some odd reason,
these words comfort you.

But what if you're the one
who, exiting the cave,
can see the world more clearly,
shadows giving way
to specks and vapors
beneath an incoherent sun?

Boston Public Garden, Early May

Tulips.
Children in three-cornered hats.

Guitarist playing badly,
voice like Orpheus.

A skeletal old man who sits
and bows his *erhu,* causing pain—

a small dog straining, taut,
so good is he, so much he wants a treat—

a young man on a swan boat
pedaling his load of souls

still in their bodies,
heading toward the bridge.

One of them looks up at me
before she passes underneath.

She has your face.

Moon Jelly at the Monterey Bay Aquarium

No blood—no bones—
no lungs—no gills—
no brain to interfere with love—

a halo of thin threads
that move in water's sway—
transparent skin,

her everything revealed.
She opens and she closes,
pulsing like a heart.

She opens and she closes
to the silent music of her grief—
a living tear.

How could a creature made of water
know that when she breaks,
she can regrow—

know that her body
holds the code for immortality?

Aran Sweater

Loose-knit of thick acrylic yarn,
in beige—"my color"—as assigned by Mother
for my brown hair and brown eyes.

She sent me brown mums every year,
not sweetheart roses like the ones she sent you
for your fine blonde hair.

So elegant on you, too small for me,
your present stretched across my lumps and bumps—
size Large, but I was larger still.

You're dead.
I'm smaller now.
The house is cold today.

I put the sweater on.
Its cable stitches running up and down
are prayers for safety,

and the diamond patterns are for health and fortune
that eluded you.
It's pilled with fuzz balls and loose threads,

but now it fits me,
and it's warm.

Things to Not Say

Don't say she's in a better place,
she's now at peace.
She isn't anywhere,
she can't experience relief.
She's not the subject of the verb "to be"
in any tense but past, or any sense but negative.
Her agony is gone, but so is she.

The brain has no machinery to feel its pain,
an ache that she, who once could lure
the wildest of words
could not communicate in anything but screams.
But that's not why she died. She fell.
Her ribs broke sharp and pierced her lungs
and drowned her like our mother
in her own heart's blood.

Don't say she didn't suffer—
how can we know her dreams?
A woman rescued from the edge of death
said she'd lain in morphine nightmares—
evil colors—oozing, dripping, uncontained—
and massing to devour her.

The air is colorless,
we barely notice it when it is clean—
we breathe unconsciously, ungratefully.
My little sister was like air to me.

I Wouldn't Have Believed It Either

I saw an angel in my bathtub,
halo lighting up the place.

She had your face—
chalcédony-and topaz eyes,

round-nostrilled nose, hair
dressed with fourteen-karat gold.

She flapped and fluttered with abandon
like a robin in a birdbath,

washing off her death and resurrection,
dripping out a secret code

to tell me spring would come again for me
as it had come for her.

Gratitude

This afternoon, my son, preoccupied and tired,
stepped out to cross the street, not thinking
that a car would hurtle toward him
from a freeway ramp.
Amazingly, he found himself transported
to the other sidewalk—safe.
He doesn't know how he survived.

I catch a glimpse of you
between the sunset clouds.
The moon relays your blessing
through a veil of fog.

Superbloom

This year brought rain.
Out of cracks between cement slabs—
out of freeway strips and even potholes—
tidal waves of flowers.

My house was made of flowers when you died—
ethereal, like you—and, like you, dead.
As children we picked flowers near a summer road.
We didn't know their names—chicory? verbena?
Queen Anne's lace?—bouquets bedraggled,
limp with yearning for the field,
and rank like fireflies we trapped in jars
for love of orange light.

Childhood was our identity,
our right, and old folks were a different breed,
although we learned that flowers die
and children, too.

I saved this season's flowers into cyberspace
and labeled them—hedgenettle, larkspur, wild geranium—
as if taxonomy and pictures could immortalize.
But words and photographs are only memory like any art,
and flowers flow from nothingness to nothingness.
They dry, feed summer fires, and flame like Northern Lights
across bad orange sky.

June 21. The date you died. Days will get shorter now.
We say the hills are "golden" though they're really brown,
the grasses on them dead—not dead like fallen leaves,
but waiting to regrow when time is right.
And Time is always right,
it's one tough customer—
the force that through the green fuse drives the flower.

Too cool for June, unseasonably gray.
The dead peek out from underneath low clouds,
their breath is fog. They wisp along the seam
that joins the sky to earth.
You are among them now.

Dialogue with Your Poems

The earth is tilting toward the sun again.
You stayed until the longest day—
the maximum of light—
the end of springtime, blue with flowers.

I love to feel the fragrance of my flesh.
Sometimes its tiny rhythms make my wrist
An animal with soft skin.

You let no rat, no ant, no fly
be killed for you.
You knew the fear
endured by fragile things.

One day the crowds will trample soft my arm
Like garbage. Who will hold me in the storm
To warm me? Where will I draw my bath?

Remember how as children we would plead
for deeper water in our tub?
Remember how you'd wash your face to rags,
the water dripping down your elbow to the floor?

As well would Andromache see sacred the ashes of her love
Seep in with the sewage of Athens, would I see mine
A peddler of erotic wares, rejected.

And I rejected you. You called me thirty times a day.
I said to call me only once. I didn't know how soon
you'd barricade yourself inside your illness,
fall, and break.

We'd chat/ of this and that—
The only way to eat chicken is with your fingers.
Yes, yes, that is the way we eat it in New York.

New York. We ran from there until the other ocean stopped us.
When we returned to cede our mother
to her sacred dead, your brain already in eclipse,
you barely cast a reddish glow.

The heavens must select/ the worthier stuff to live.
And then I felt / All sacrificial, bound to die instead
Of better, stronger things, instead of you.

Celebration of Life

You have evaporated from the slide show
like an old perfume.

Picture after picture flashes by—

girl hiding braces with a tight-lipped smile—

bride in white with stephanotis—

bride in blue,

a crown of roses sparked with baby's breath—

old woman wilted on an old man's shoulder, giving in.

Enter my foolish ghost, I acquiesce . . .
and Nothingness becomes its own caress.

Have you discovered
only Nothingness?

Your name was Dolly Gordon.
Now your name
is scouring the shrubbery for you, the clouds.
Not finding you, it wastes away.

You are a blossom dried and pressed,
flaking into stardust

spreading out into the Nothing
and the Everything,

contained in all the living flowers.

Even myself reminds me of you

—Lucie Brock-Broido

Two sisters died today,
conjoined at the temples, facing different ways.
On YouTube they are dancing in a field.
The larger swirls the smaller on a swivel seat,
whirls her over grass, around the trees,
a single dance, a single song,
a single passage to the place you are, alone.

Impossible to understand: you're gone.

Is Heaven one big consciousness
so pure it glows, one vast aurora
that reveals itself from time to time?
Am I invisible to you, mysterious,
as you to me?
My life span forms parentheses around your life,
the sentence going on.

Final Instructions

do not bury her
already buried. flute
of ebony and silver.
music ribbon knotted to a nut.
soft-stringed guitar.
throat's arioso throttled song garroted

deep-buried blackberry not tasted
wasted picked plucked tucked away.
unripened grape unpressed. oak-aged
in darkness. intoxicating
no one

do not bury her already buried.
burn away her reliquary. gaze amazed

Cremation

No bamboo pyre, no ritual,
no prayer, just heat.

The sieve
that later sifts the ashes

for left-over things
like wedding rings,

is not set up to recognize
the soul blown open

like a pine cone needing fire
to release its seeds.

Notes

"*Into the raw mottled air of a dim bedroom.*" Italicized lines are from Psalms 6:6 KJV and John 14:18 KJV.

"Close of Day." "*Do not go gentle*" is from Dylan Thomas' poem.

"Floodlit." Italicized lines are from spoken words and poetry by Dolly Garter Gordon, used with permission.

"Superbloom." "*The force that through the green fuse drives the flower*" is from Dylan Thomas' poem.

"Dialogue With My Sister's Poems on the First Anniversary of Her Death." Italicized stanzas are from poems by Dolly Garter Gordon, quoted with permission.

"Celebration of Life." Italicized lines are from a poem by Dolly Garter Gordon, published in *The Advocate* in the 1960s.

About the Author

Joyce Schmid is a grandmother and psychotherapist living in Palo Alto, California, with her husband of over half a century. After graduation from Harvard College in History and Literature, she studied Russian Literature at Columbia Graduate School where she was twice awarded their Pushkin Prize for poetry translation. She then earned a Ph.D., in Clinical Psychology from the Pacific Graduate School of Psychology (now Palo Alto University).

Her poems have most recently appeared in *Bridport Prize Anthology 2025, The Hudson Review, The Orchards Poetry Journal, New Ohio Review, Passager, Salt,* and other journals and anthologies. Her chapbook is *Natural Science* (Glass Lyre Press, 2025).

When Joyce's younger sister Dolly was an undergraduate at Harvard, she was admitted to a coveted poetry workshop taught by Robert Lowell, who admired her poetry. After it ended, Dolly never wrote poetry again. In Dolly's last years, Joyce asked her if she could quote those poems in her own work. "Please do," she answered. "Maybe that way someone will see them." Accordingly, some of the poems in this chapbook contain Dolly's beautiful words.

www.ingramcontent.com/pod-product-compliance
Lightning Source LLC
LaVergne TN
LVHW090538110826
845146LV00003B/1162

* 9 7 9 8 9 0 1 4 6 7 2 4 4 *